T. S. Eliot: A New Collection

T. S. Eliot
A New Collection

Includes The Waste Land, Prufrock, and two other classic volumes of Eliot's poems, plus previously uncollected poetry

T. S. Eliot

Stonewell Press

ISBN 978-1-62730-039-1

The views expressed in this book are the responsibility of the author and do not necessarily represent the position of Stonewell Press. The reader alone is responsible for the use of any ideas or information provided by this book.

Published by Stonewell Press, Salt Lake City, Utah.

www.stonewellpress.com
editor@stonewellpress.com

Contents

The Early Poems

Song

When we came home across the hill
  No leaves were fallen from the trees;
The gentle fingers of the breeze
  Had torn no quivering cobweb down.
The hedgerow bloomed with flowers still,
  No withered petals lay beneath;
But the wild roses in your wreath
  Were faded, and the leaves were brown.

Song

If space and time, as sages say,
   Are things which cannot be,
The fly that lives a single day
   Has lived as long as we.
But let us live while yet we may,
   While love and life are free,
For time is time, and runs away,
   Though sages disagree.

The flowers I sent thee when the dew
   Was trembling on the vine,
Were withered ere the wild bee flew
   To suck the eglantine.
But let us haste to pluck anew
   Nor mourn to see them pine,
And though the flowers of love be few
   Yet let them be divine.

Before Morning

While all the East was weaving red with gray,
The flowers at the window turned toward dawn,
Petal on petal, waiting for the day,
Fresh flowers, withered flowers, flowers of dawn.

This morning's flowers and flowers of yesterday
Their fragrance drifts across the room at dawn,
Fragrance of bloom and fragrance of decay,
Fresh flowers, withered flowers, flowers of dawn.

Circe's Palace

Around her fountain which flows
With the voice of men in pain,
Are flowers that no man knows.
Their petals are fanged and red
With hideous streak and stain.
They sprang from the limbs of the dead.—
We shall not come here again.

Panthers rise from their lairs
In the forest which thickens below,
Along the garden stairs
The sluggish python lies;
The peacock's walk, stately and slow
And they look at us with the eyes
Of men whom we knew long ago.

On a Portrait

Among a crowd of tenuous dreams, unknown
To us of restless brain and weary feet,
Forever hurrying, up and down the street,
She stands at evening in the room alone.

Not like a tranquil goddess carved of stone
But evanescent, as if one should meet
A pensive lamia in some wood-retreat,
An immaterial fancy of one's own.

No meditations glad or ominous
Disturb her lips, or move the slender hands;
Her dark eyes keep their secrets hid from us,
Beyond the circle of our thoughts she stands.

The parrot on the bar, a silent spy,
Regards her with a patient curious eye.

Song

The moonflower opens to the moth,
   The mist crawls in from sea;
A great white bird, a snowy owl,
   Slips from the alder tree.

Whiter the flowers, love, you hold,
   Than the white mist on the sea;
Have you no brighter tropic flowers
   With scarlet life, for me?

Nocturne

Romeo, *grand sérieux,* to importune
Guitar and hat in hand, beside the gate
With Juliet, in the usual debate
Of love, beneath a bored but courteous moon;
The conversation failing, strikes some tune
Banal, and out of pity for their fate
Behind the wall I have some servant wait,
Stab, and the lady sinks into a swoon.

Blood looks effective on the moonlit ground—
The hero smiles; in my best mode oblique
Rolls toward the moon a frenzied eye profound,
(No need of "Love forever?"—"Love next week?")
While female readers all in tears are drowned:—
"The perfect climax all true lovers seek!"

Humouresque

(After J. Laforgue)

One of my marionettes is dead
Though not yet tired of the game—
But weak in body as in head,
(A jumping-jack has such a frame).

But this deceaséd marionette
I rather liked: a common face,
(The kind of face that we forget)
Pinched in a comic, dull grimace;

Half bullying, half imploring air,
Mouth twisted to the latest tune;
His who-the-devil-are-you stare;
Translated, maybe, to the moon.

With Limbo's other useless things
Haranguing spectres, set him there;
"The snappiest fashion since last spring's,
"The newest style, on Earth, I swear.

"Why don't you people get some class?
(Feebly contemptuous of nose),
"Your damned thin moonlight, worse than gas—
"Now in New York"—and so it goes.

Logic a marionette's, all wrong
Of premises; yet in some star
A hero!—Where would he belong?
But, even at that, what mask *bizarre!*

Spleen

Sunday: this satisfied procession
Of definite Sunday faces;
Bonnets, silk hats, and conscious graces
In repetition that displaces
Your mental self-possession
By this unwarranted digression.

Evening, lights, and tea!
Children and cats in the alley;
Dejection unable to rally
Against this dull conspiracy.

And Life, a little bald and gray,
Languid, fastidious, and bland,
Waits, hat and gloves in hand,
Punctilious of tie and suit
(Somewhat impatient of delay)
On the doorstep of the Absolute.

Ode

For the hour that is left us Fair Harvard, with thee,
   Ere we face the importunate years,
In thy shadow we wait, while thy presence dispels
   Our vain hesitations and fears.
And we turn as thy sons ever turn, in the strength
   Of the hopes that thy blessings bestow,
From the hopes and ambitions that sprang at thy feet
   To the thoughts of the past as we go.

Yet for all of these years that to-morrow has lost
   We are still the less able to grieve,
With so much that of Harvard we carry away
   In the place of the life that we leave.
And only the years that efface and destroy
   Give us also the vision to see
What we owe for the future, the present, and past,
   Fair Harvard, to thine and to thee.

Uncollected Poems

Song to the Opherian

The golden foot I may not kiss or clutch
Glowed in the shadow of the bed
Perhaps it does not come to very much
This thought this ghost this pendulum in the head
Swinging from life to death
Bleeding between two lives
            Waiting that touch.

The wind sprang up and broke the bells,
Is it a dream or something else
When the surface of the blackened river
Is a face that sweats with tears?
I saw across the alien river
The campfire shake the spears.

GUS KRUTZSCH.[1]

1. This is a pseudonym Eliot used

Ode

To you particularly, and to all the Volscians
Great hurt and mischief.

Tired.
Subterrene laughter synchronous
With silence from the sacred wood
And bubbling of the uninspired
Mephitic river.
                    Misunderstood
The accents of the now retired
Profession of the calamus.

Tortured.
When the bridegroom smoothed his hair
There was blood upon the bed.
Morning was already late.
Children singing in the orchard
(Io Hymen, Hymenaee)
Succuba eviscerate.

Tortuous.
By arrangement with Perseus
The fooled resentment of the dragon
Sailing before the wind at dawn
Golden apocalypse. Indignant

At the cheap extinction of his taking-off.
Now lies he there
Tip to tip washed beneath Charles' Wagon.

Prufrock
and Other Observations

Or puoi la quantitate
comprender dell' amor ch'a te mi scalda,
quando dismento nostra vanitate,
trattando l'ombre come cosa salda.

The Love Song of J. Alfred Prufrock

S'io credesse che mia risposta fosse
A persona che mai tornasse al mondo,
Questa fiamma staria senza piu scosse.
Ma perciocche giammai di questo fondo
Non torno vivo alcun, s'i'odo il vero,
Senza tema d'infamia ti rispondo.

Let us go then, you and I,
When the evening is spread out against the sky
Like a patient etherised upon a table;
Let us go, through certain half-deserted streets,
The muttering retreats
Of restless nights in one-night cheap hotels
And sawdust restaurants with oyster-shells:
Streets that follow like a tedious argument
Of insidious intent
To lead you to an overwhelming question . . .
Oh, do not ask, "What is it?"
Let us go and make our visit.

In the room the women come and go
Talking of Michelangelo.

The yellow fog that rubs its back upon the window-panes,
The yellow smoke that rubs its muzzle on the window-panes

Licked its tongue into the corners of the evening,
Lingered upon the pools that stand in drains,
Let fall upon its back the soot that falls from chimneys,
Slipped by the terrace, made a sudden leap,
And seeing that it was a soft October night,
Curled once about the house, and fell asleep.

And indeed there will be time
For the yellow smoke that slides along the street,
Rubbing its back upon the window-panes;
There will be time, there will be time
To prepare a face to meet the faces that you meet;
There will be time to murder and create,
And time for all the works and days of hands
That lift and drop a question on your plate;
Time for you and time for me,
And time yet for a hundred indecisions,
And for a hundred visions and revisions,
Before the taking of a toast and tea.

In the room the women come and go
Talking of Michelangelo.

And indeed there will be time
To wonder, "Do I dare?" and, "Do I dare?"
Time to turn back and descend the stair,
With a bald spot in the middle of my hair—
[They will say: "How his hair is growing thin!"]
My morning coat, my collar mounting firmly to the chin,
My necktie rich and modest, but asserted by a simple pin—
[They will say: "But how his arms and legs are thin!"]
Do I dare
Disturb the universe?

In a minute there is time
For decisions and revisions which a minute will reverse.

  For I have known them all already, known them all:—
Have known the evenings, mornings, afternoons,
I have measured out my life with coffee spoons;
I know the voices dying with a dying fall
Beneath the music from a farther room.
  So how should I presume?

  And I have known the eyes already, known them all—
The eyes that fix you in a formulated phrase,
And when I am formulated, sprawling on a pin,
When I am pinned and wriggling on the wall,
Then how should I begin
To spit out all the butt-ends of my days and ways?
  And how should I presume?

  And I have known the arms already, known them all—
Arms that are braceleted and white and bare
[But in the lamplight, downed with light brown hair!]
Is it perfume from a dress
That makes me so digress?
Arms that lie along a table, or wrap about a shawl.
  And should I then presume?
  And how should I begin?

. . . . .

Shall I say, I have gone at dusk through narrow streets
And watched the smoke that rises from the pipes
Of lonely men in shirt-sleeves, leaning out of windows? . . .

I should have been a pair of ragged claws
Scuttling across the floors of silent seas.

. . . . .

And the afternoon, the evening, sleeps so peacefully!
Smoothed by long fingers,
Asleep . . . tired . . . or it malingers,
Stretched on the floor, here beside you and me.
Should I, after tea and cakes and ices,
Have the strength to force the moment to its crisis?
But though I have wept and fasted, wept and prayed,
Though I have seen my head [grown slightly bald] brought in
upon a platter,
I am no prophet—and here's no great matter;
I have seen the moment of my greatness flicker,
And I have seen the eternal Footman hold my coat, and
snicker,
And in short, I was afraid.

And would it have been worth it, after all,
After the cups, the marmalade, the tea,
Among the porcelain, among some talk of you and me,
Would it have been worth while,
To have bitten off the matter with a smile,
To have squeezed the universe into a ball
To roll it toward some overwhelming question,
To say: "I am Lazarus, come from the dead,
Come back to tell you all, I shall tell you all"—
If one, settling a pillow by her head,
Should say: "That is not what I meant at all.
That is not it, at all."

And would it have been worth it, after all,
Would it have been worth while,
After the sunsets and the dooryards and the sprinkled streets,
After the novels, after the teacups, after the skirts that trail along the floor—
And this, and so much more?—
It is impossible to say just what I mean!
But as if a magic lantern threw the nerves in patterns on a screen:
Would it have been worth while
If one, settling a pillow or throwing off a shawl,
And turning toward the window, should say:
"That is not it at all,
That is not what I meant, at all."

. . . . .

No! I am not Prince Hamlet, nor was meant to be;
Am an attendant lord, one that will do
To swell a progress, start a scene or two,
Advise the prince; no doubt, an easy tool,
Deferential, glad to be of use,
Politic, cautious, and meticulous;
Full of high sentence, but a bit obtuse;
At times, indeed, almost ridiculous—
Almost, at times, the Fool.

I grow old . . . I grow old . . .
I shall wear the bottoms of my trousers rolled.

Shall I part my hair behind? Do I dare to eat a peach?
I shall wear white flannel trousers, and walk upon the beach.
I have heard the mermaids singing, each to each.

I do not think that they will sing to me.

I have seen them riding seaward on the waves
Combing the white hair of the waves blown back
When the wind blows the water white and black.

We have lingered in the chambers of the sea
By sea-girls wreathed with seaweed red and brown
Till human voices wake us, and we drown.

Portrait of a Lady

Thou hast committed—
Fornication: but that was in another country,
And besides, the wench is dead.

The Jew of Malta

I

Among the smoke and fog of a December afternoon
You have the scene arrange itself—as it will seem to do—
With "I have saved this afternoon for you";
And four wax candles in the darkened room,
Four rings of light upon the ceiling overhead,
An atmosphere of Juliet's tomb
Prepared for all the things to be said, or left unsaid.
We have been, let us say, to hear the latest Pole
Transmit the Preludes, through his hair and fingertips.
"So intimate, this Chopin, that I think his soul
Should be resurrected only among friends
Some two or three, who will not touch the bloom
That is rubbed and questioned in the concert room."
—And so the conversation slips
Among velleities and carefully caught regrets
Through attenuated tones of violins
Mingled with remote cornets

And begins.
"You do not know how much they mean to me, my friends,
And how, how rare and strange it is, to find
In a life composed so much, so much of odds and ends,
[For indeed I do not love it ... you knew? you are not blind!
How keen you are!]
To find a friend who has these qualities,
Who has, and gives
Those qualities upon which friendship lives.
How much it means that I say this to you—
Without these friendships—life, what *cauchemar!*"

Among the windings of the violins
And the ariettes
Of cracked cornets
Inside my brain a dull tom-tom begins
Absurdly hammering a prelude of its own,
Capricious monotone
That is at least one definite "false note."
—Let us take the air, in a tobacco trance,
Admire the monuments,
Discuss the late events,
Correct our watches by the public clocks.
Then sit for half an hour and drink our bocks.

II

Now that lilacs are in bloom
She has a bowl of lilacs in her room
And twists one in her fingers while she talks.
"Ah, my friend, you do not know, you do not know
What life is, you who hold it in your hands";

(Slowly twisting the lilac stalks)
"You let it flow from you, you let it flow,
And youth is cruel, and has no remorse
And smiles at situations which it cannot see."
I smile, of course,
And go on drinking tea.
"Yet with these April sunsets, that somehow recall
My buried life, and Paris in the Spring,
I feel immeasurably at peace, and find the world
To be wonderful and youthful, after all."

The voice returns like the insistent out-of-tune
Of a broken violin on an August afternoon:
"I am always sure that you understand
My feelings, always sure that you feel,
Sure that across the gulf you reach your hand.

You are invulnerable, you have no Achilles' heel.
You will go on, and when you have prevailed
You can say: at this point many a one has failed.

But what have I, but what have I, my friend,
To give you, what can you receive from me?
Only the friendship and the sympathy
Of one about to reach her journey's end.

I shall sit here, serving tea to friends. . . ."

I take my hat: how can I make a cowardly amends
For what she has said to me?
You will see me any morning in the park
Reading the comics and the sporting page.
Particularly I remark
An English countess goes upon the stage.

A Greek was murdered at a Polish dance,
Another bank defaulter has confessed.
I keep my countenance,
I remain self-possessed
Except when a street piano, mechanical and tired
Reiterates some worn-out common song
With the smell of hyacinths across the garden
Recalling things that other people have desired.
Are these ideas right or wrong?

III

The October night comes down; returning as before
Except for a slight sensation of being ill at ease
I mount the stairs and turn the handle of the door
And feel as if I had mounted on my hands and knees.
"And so you are going abroad; and when do you return?
But that's a useless question.
You hardly know when you are coming back,
You will find so much to learn."
My smile falls heavily among the bric-à-brac.

"Perhaps you can write to me."
My self-possession flares up for a second;
This is as I had reckoned.
"I have been wondering frequently of late
(But our beginnings never know our ends!)
Why we have not developed into friends."
I feel like one who smiles, and turning shall remark
Suddenly, his expression in a glass.
My self-possession gutters; we are really in the dark.

"For everybody said so, all our friends,

They all were sure our feelings would relate
So closely! I myself can hardly understand.
We must leave it now to fate.
You will write, at any rate.
Perhaps it is not too late.
I shall sit here, serving tea to friends."

And I must borrow every changing shape
To find expression . . . dance, dance
Like a dancing bear,
Cry like a parrot, chatter like an ape.
Let us take the air, in a tobacco trance—

Well! and what if she should die some afternoon,
Afternoon grey and smoky, evening yellow and rose;
Should die and leave me sitting pen in hand
With the smoke coming down above the housetops;
Doubtful, for a while
Not knowing what to feel or if I understand
Or whether wise or foolish, tardy or too soon...
Would she not have the advantage, after all?
This music is successful with a "dying fall"
Now that we talk of dying—
And should I have the right to smile?

Preludes

I

The winter evening settles down
With smell of steaks in passageways.
Six o'clock.
The burnt-out ends of smoky days.
And now a gusty shower wraps
The grimy scraps
Of withered leaves about your feet
And newspapers from vacant lots;
The showers beat
On broken blinds and chimney-pots,
And at the corner of the street
A lonely cab-horse steams and stamps.
And then the lighting of the lamps.

II

The morning comes to consciousness
Of faint stale smells of beer
From the sawdust-trampled street
With all its muddy feet that press
To early coffee-stands.
With the other masquerades

That time resumes,
One thinks of all the hands
That are raising dingy shades
In a thousand furnished rooms.

III

You tossed a blanket from the bed,
You lay upon your back, and waited;
You dozed, and watched the night revealing
The thousand sordid images
Of which your soul was constituted;
They flickered against the ceiling.
And when all the world came back
And the light crept up between the shutters
And you heard the sparrows in the gutters,
You had such a vision of the street
As the street hardly understands;
Sitting along the bed's edge, where
You curled the papers from your hair,
Or clasped the yellow soles of feet
In the palms of both soiled hands.

IV

His soul stretched tight across the skies
That fade behind a city block,
Or trampled by insistent feet
At four and five and six o'clock;
And short square fingers stuffing pipes,
And evening newspapers, and eyes

Assured of certain certainties,
The conscience of a blackened street
Impatient to assume the world.

I am moved by fancies that are curled
Around these images, and cling:
The notion of some infinitely gentle
Infinitely suffering thing.

Wipe your hand across your mouth, and laugh;
The worlds revolve like ancient women
Gathering fuel in vacant lots.

Rhapsody on a Windy Night

Twelve o'clock.
Along the reaches of the street
Held in a lunar synthesis,
Whispering lunar incantations
Dissolve the floors of memory
And all its clear relations,
Its divisions and precisions,
Every street lamp that I pass
Beats like a fatalistic drum,
And through the spaces of the dark
Midnight shakes the memory
As a madman shakes a dead geranium.

Half-past one,
The street-lamp sputtered,
The street-lamp muttered,
The street-lamp said, "Regard that woman
Who hesitates toward you in the light of the door
Which opens on her like a grin.
You see the border of her dress
Is torn and stained with sand,
And you see the corner of her eye
Twists like a crooked pin."

The memory throws up high and dry
A crowd of twisted things;
A twisted branch upon the beach
Eaten smooth, and polished
As if the world gave up
The secret of its skeleton,
Stiff and white.
A broken spring in a factory yard,
Rust that clings to the form that the strength has left
Hard and curled and ready to snap.

Half-past two,
The street-lamp said,
"Remark the cat which flattens itself in the gutter,
Slips out its tongue
And devours a morsel of rancid butter."
So the hand of the child, automatic,
Slipped out and pocketed a toy that was running along the quay.
I could see nothing behind that child's eye.
I have seen eyes in the street
Trying to peer through lighted shutters,
And a crab one afternoon in a pool,
An old crab with barnacles on his back,
Gripped the end of a stick which I held him.

Half-past three,
The lamp sputtered,
The lamp muttered in the dark.
The lamp hummed:
"Regard the moon,
La lune ne garde aucune rancune,
She winks a feeble eye,

She smiles into corners.
She smooths the hair of the grass.
The moon has lost her memory.
A washed-out smallpox cracks her face,
Her hand twists a paper rose,
That smells of dust and eau de Cologne,
She is alone
With all the old nocturnal smells
That cross and cross across her brain."
The reminiscence comes
Of sunless dry geraniums
And dust in crevices,
Smells of chestnuts in the streets,
And female smells in shuttered rooms,
And cigarettes in corridors
And cocktail smells in bars.

The lamp said,
"Four o'clock,
Here is the number on the door.
Memory!
You have the key,
The little lamp spreads a ring on the stair.
Mount.
The bed is open; the tooth-brush hangs on the wall,
Put your shoes at the door, sleep, prepare for life."

The last twist of the knife.

Morning at the Window

They are rattling breakfast plates in basement kitchens,
And along the trampled edges of the street
I am aware of the damp souls of housemaids
Sprouting despondently at area gates.

The brown waves of fog toss up to me
Twisted faces from the bottom of the street,
And tear from a passer-by with muddy skirts
An aimless smile that hovers in the air
And vanishes along the level of the roofs.

The *Boston Evening Transcript*

The readers of the *Boston Evening Transcript*
Sway in the wind like a field of ripe corn.

When evening quickens faintly in the street,
Wakening the appetites of life in some
And to others bringing the *Boston Evening Transcript,*
I mount the steps and ring the bell, turning
Wearily, as one would turn to nod good-bye to
Rochefoucauld,
If the street were time and he at the end of the street,
And I say, "Cousin Harriet, here is the *Boston Evening*
Transcript.

Aunt Helen

Miss Helen Slingsby was my maiden aunt,
And lived in a small house near a fashionable square
Cared for by servants to the number of four.
Now when she died there was silence in heaven
And silence at her end of the street.
The shutters were drawn and the undertaker wiped his feet—
He was aware that this sort of thing had occurred before.
The dogs were handsomely provided for,
But shortly afterwards the parrot died too.
The Dresden clock continued ticking on the mantelpiece,
And the footman sat upon the dining-table
Holding the second housemaid on his knees—
Who had always been so careful while her mistress lived.

Cousin Nancy

Miss Nancy Ellicott
Strode across the hills and broke them,
Rode across the hills and broke them—
The barren New England hills—
Riding to hounds
Over the cow-pasture.

Miss Nancy Ellicott smoked
And danced all the modern dances;
And her aunts were not quite sure how they felt about it,
But they knew that it was modern.

Upon the glazen shelves kept watch
Matthew and Waldo, guardians of the faith,
The army of unalterable law.

Mr. Apollinax

Ω τῆς καινότητος. Ἡράκλεις, τῆς παραδοξολογίας.
εὐμήχανος ἄνθρωπος.

Lucian

When Mr. Apollinax visited the United States
His laughter tinkled among the teacups.
I thought of Fragilion, that shy figure among the birch-trees,
And of Priapus in the shrubbery
Gaping at the lady in the swing.
In the palace of Mrs. Phlaccus, at Professor
  Channing-Cheetah's
He laughed like an irresponsible foetus.
His laughter was submarine and profound
Like the old man of the sea's
Hidden under coral islands
Where worried bodies of drowned men drift down in the
  green silence,
Dropping from fingers of surf.
I looked for the head of Mr. Apollinax rolling under a chair

  Or grinning over a screen
With seaweed in its hair.
I heard the beat of centaur's hoofs over the hard turf
As his dry and passionate talk devoured the afternoon.

"He is a charming man"—"But after all what did he
mean?"—
"His pointed ears. . . . He must be unbalanced,"—
"There was something he said that I might have challenged."
Of dowager Mrs. Phlaccus, and Professor and Mrs. Cheetah
I remember a slice of lemon, and a bitten macaroon.

Hysteria

As she laughed I was aware of becoming involved in her laughter and being part of it, until her teeth were only accidental stars with a talent for squad-drill. I was drawn in by short gasps, inhaled at each momentary recovery, lost finally in the dark caverns of her throat, bruised by the ripple of unseen muscles. An elderly waiter with trembling hands was hurriedly spreading a pink and white checked cloth over the rusty green iron table, saying: "If the lady and gentleman wish to take their tea in the garden, if the lady and gentleman wish to take their tea in the garden . . ." I decided that if the shaking of her breasts could be stopped, some of the fragments of the afternoon might be collected, and I concentrated my attention with careful subtlety to this end.

Conversation Galante

I observe: "Our sentimental friend the moon!
Or possibly (fantastic, I confess)
It may be Prester John's balloon
Or an old battered lantern hung aloft
To light poor travellers to their distress."
  She then: "How you digress!"

And I then: "Someone frames upon the keys
That exquisite nocturne, with which we explain
The night and moonshine; music which we seize
To body forth our own vacuity."
  She then: "Does this refer to me?"
  "Oh no, it is I who am inane."

"You, madam, are the eternal humorist,
The eternal enemy of the absolute,
Giving our vagrant moods the slightest twist!
With your air indifferent and imperious
At a stroke our mad poetics to confute—"
  And—"Are we then so serious?"

La Figlia che Piange

O quam te memorem virgo . . .

Stand on the highest pavement of the stair—
Lean on a garden urn—
Weave, weave the sunlight in your hair—
Clasp your flowers to you with a pained surprise—
Fling them to the ground and turn
With a fugitive resentment in your eyes:
But weave, weave the sunlight in your hair.

So I would have had him leave,
So I would have had her stand and grieve,
So he would have left
As the soul leaves the body torn and bruised,
As the mind deserts the body it has used.
I should find
Some way incomparably light and deft,
Some way we both should understand,
Simple and faithless as a smile and shake of the hand.

She turned away, but with the autumn weather
Compelled my imagination many days,
Many days and many hours:
Her hair over her arms and her arms full of flowers.

And I wonder how they should have been together!
I should have lost a gesture and a pose.
Sometimes these cogitations still amaze
The troubled midnight and the noon's repose.

Poems 1920

Gerontion

Thou hast nor youth nor age
But as it were an after dinner sleep
Dreaming of both.

Here I am, an old man in a dry month,
Being read to by a boy, waiting for rain.
I was neither at the hot gates
Nor fought in the warm rain
Nor knee deep in the salt marsh, heaving a cutlass,
Bitten by flies, fought.
My house is a decayed house,
And the jew squats on the window sill, the owner,
Spawned in some estaminet of Antwerp,
Blistered in Brussels, patched and peeled in London.
The goat coughs at night in the field overhead;
Rocks, moss, stonecrop, iron, merds.
The woman keeps the kitchen, makes tea,
Sneezes at evening, poking the peevish gutter.
I an old man,
A dull head among windy spaces.

Signs are taken for wonders. "We would see a sign!"
The word within a word, unable to speak a word,
Swaddled with darkness. In the juvescence of the year

Came Christ the tiger

In depraved May, dogwood and chestnut, flowering judas,
To be eaten, to be divided, to be drunk
Among whispers; by Mr. Silvero
With caressing hands, at Limoges
Who walked all night in the next room;
By Hakagawa, bowing among the Titians;
By Madame de Tornquist, in the dark room
Shifting the candles; Fräulein von Kulp
Who turned in the hall, one hand on the door. Vacant shuttles
Weave the wind. I have no ghosts,
An old man in a draughty house
Under a windy knob.

After such knowledge, what forgiveness? Think now
History has many cunning passages, contrived corridors
And issues, deceives with whispering ambitions,
Guides us by vanities. Think now
She gives when our attention is distracted
And what she gives, gives with such supple confusions
That the giving famishes the craving. Gives too late
What's not believed in, or if still believed,
In memory only, reconsidered passion. Gives too soon
Into weak hands, what's thought can be dispensed with
Till the refusal propagates a fear. Think
Neither fear nor courage saves us. Unnatural vices
Are fathered by our heroism. Virtues
Are forced upon us by our impudent crimes.
These tears are shaken from the wrath-bearing tree.

The tiger springs in the new year. Us he devours. Think at last
We have not reached conclusion, when I
Stiffen in a rented house. Think at last
I have not made this show purposelessly
And it is not by any concitation
Of the backward devils.

I would meet you upon this honestly.
I that was near your heart was removed therefrom
To lose beauty in terror, terror in inquisition.
I have lost my passion: why should I need to keep it
Since what is kept must be adulterated?
I have lost my sight, smell, hearing, taste and touch:
How should I use them for your closer contact?

These with a thousand small deliberations
Protract the profit of their chilled delirium,
Excite the membrane, when the sense has cooled,
With pungent sauces, multiply variety
In a wilderness of mirrors. What will the spider do,
Suspend its operations, will the weevil
Delay? De Bailhache, Fresca, Mrs. Cammel, whirled
Beyond the circuit of the shuddering Bear
In fractured atoms. Gull against the wind, in the windy straits
Of Belle Isle, or running on the Horn,
White feathers in the snow, the Gulf claims,
And an old man driven by the Trades
To a sleepy corner.

Tenants of the house,
Thoughts of a dry brain in a dry season.

Burbank with a Baedeker: Bleistein with a Cigar

Tra-la-la-la-la-la-laire—nil nisi divinum stabile est; caetera fumus—the gondola stopped, the old palace was there, how charming its grey and pink—goats and monkeys, with such hair too!—so the countess passed on until she came through the little park, where Niobe presented her with a cabinet, and so departed.

Burbank crossed a little bridge
  Descending at a small hotel;
Princess Volupine arrived,
  They were together, and he fell.

Defunctive music under sea
  Passed seaward with the passing bell
Slowly: the God Hercules
  Had left him, that had loved him well.

The horses, under the axletree
  Beat up the dawn from Istria
With even feet. Her shuttered barge
  Burned on the water all the day.

But this or such was Bleistein's way:
  A saggy bending of the knees
And elbows, with the palms turned out,
  Chicago Semite Viennese.

A lustreless protrusive eye
   Stares from the protozoic slime
At a perspective of Canaletto.
   The smoky candle end of time

Declines. On the Rialto once.
   The rats are underneath the piles.
The jew is underneath the lot.
   Money in furs. The boatman smiles,

Princess Volupine extends
   A meagre, blue-nailed, phthisic hand
To climb the waterstair. Lights, lights,
   She entertains Sir Ferdinand

Klein. Who clipped the lion's wings
   And flea'd his rump and pared his claws?
Thought Burbank, meditating on
   Time's ruins, and the seven laws.

Sweeney Erect

And the trees about me,
Let them be dry and leafless; let the rocks
Groan with continual surges; and behind me
Make all a desolation. Look, look, wenches!

Paint me a cavernous waste shore
Cast in the unstilled Cyclades,
Paint me the bold anfractuous rocks
Faced by the snarled and yelping seas.

Display me Aeolus above
Reviewing the insurgent gales
Which tangle Ariadne's hair
And swell with haste the perjured sails.

Morning stirs the feet and hands
(Nausicaa and Polypheme).
Gesture of orang-outang
Rises from the sheets in steam.

This withered root of knots of hair
Slitted below and gashed with eyes,
This oval O cropped out with teeth:
The sickle motion from the thighs

Jackknifes upward at the knees
  Then straightens out from heel to hip
Pushing the framework of the bed
  And clawing at the pillow slip.

Sweeney addressed full length to shave
  Broadbottomed, pink from nape to base,
Knows the female temperament
  And wipes the suds around his face.

(The lengthened shadow of a man
  Is history, said Emerson
Who had not seen the silhouette
  Of Sweeney straddled in the sun.)

Tests the razor on his leg
  Waiting until the shriek subsides.
The epileptic on the bed
  Curves backward, clutching at her sides.

The ladies of the corridor
  Find themselves involved, disgraced,
Call witness to their principles
  And deprecate the lack of taste

Observing that hysteria
  Might easily be misunderstood;
Mrs. Turner intimates
  It does the house no sort of good.

But Doris, towelled from the bath,
  Enters padding on broad feet,
Bringing sal volatile
  And a glass of brandy neat.

A Cooking Egg

En l'an trentiesme do mon aage
Que toutes mes hontes j'ay beues . . .

Pipit sate upright in her chair
  Some distance from where I was sitting;
Views of the Oxford Colleges
  Lay on the table, with the knitting.

Daguerreotypes and silhouettes,
  Here grandfather and great great aunts,
Supported on the mantelpiece
  An *Invitation to the Dance.*

. . . . .

I shall not want Honour in Heaven
  For I shall meet Sir Philip Sidney
And have talk with Coriolanus
  And other heroes of that kidney.

I shall not want Capital in Heaven
  For I shall meet Sir Alfred Mond.
We two shall lie together, lapt
  In a five per cent. Exchequer Bond.

I shall not want Society in Heaven,
   Lucretia Borgia shall be my Bride;
Her anecdotes will be more amusing
   Than Pipit's experience could provide.

I shall not want Pipit in Heaven:
   Madame Blavatsky will instruct me
In the Seven Sacred Trances;
   Piccarda de Donati will conduct me.

. . . . .

But where is the penny world I bought
   To eat with Pipit behind the screen?
The red-eyed scavengers are creeping
   From Kentish Town and Golder's Green;

Where are the eagles and the trumpets?

   Buried beneath some snow-deep Alps.
Over buttered scones and crumpets
   Weeping, weeping multitudes
Droop in a hundred A.B.C.'s.

[Editor's note: ABC's refers to "Aerated Bread Company, Limited," or the many teashops found in London.]

Le Directeur

Malheur à la malheureuse Tamise
Qui coule si près du Spectateur.
Le directeur
Conservateur
Du Spectateur
Empeste la brise.
Les actionnaires
Réactionnaires
Du Spectateur
Conservateur
Bras dessus bras dessous
Font des tours
A pas de loup.
Dans un égout
Une petite fille
En guenilles
Camarde
Regarde
Le directeur
Du Spectateur
Conservateur
Et crève d'amour.

Mélange Adultère de Tout

En Amerique, professeur;
En Angleterre, journaliste;
C'est à grands pas et en sueur
Que vous suivrez à peine ma piste.
En Yorkshire, conférencier;
A Londres, un peu banquier,
Vous me paierez bein la tête.
C'est à Paris que je me coiffe
Casque noir de jemenfoutiste.
En Allemagne, philosophe
Surexcité par Emporheben
Au grand air de Bergsteigleben;
J'erre toujours de-ci de-là
A divers coups de tra là là
De Damas jusqu'à Omaha.
Je célébrai mon jour de fête
Dans une oasis d'Afrique
Vêtu d'une peau de girafe.

On montrera mon cénotaphe
Aux côtes brûlantes de Mozambique.

Lune de Miel

Ils ont vu les Pays-Bas, ils rentrent à Terre Haute;
Mais une nuit d'été, les voici à Ravenne,
A l'aise entre deux draps, chez deux centaines de punaises;
La sueur aestivale, et une forte odeur de chienne.
Ils restent sur le dos écartant les genoux
De quatre jambes molles tout gonflées de morsures.
On relève le drap pour mieux égratigner.
Moins d'une lieue d'ici est Saint Apollinaire
En Classe, basilique connue des amateurs
De chapitaux d'acanthe que tournoie le vent.

Ils vont prendre le train de huit heures
Prolonger leurs misères de Padoue à Milan
Où se trouvent la Cène, et un restaurant pas cher.
Lui pense aux pourboires, et rédige son bilan.
Ils auront vu la Suisse et traversé la France.
Et Saint Apollinaire, raide et ascétique,
Vieille usine désaffectée de Dieu, tient encore
Dans ses pierres écroulantes la forme précise de Byzance.

The Hippopotamus

Similiter et omnes revereantur Diaconos, ut mandatum Jesu Christi; et Episcopum, ut Jesum Christum, existentem filium Patris; Presbyteros autem, ut concilium Dei et conjunctionem Apostolorum. Sine his Ecclesia non vocatur; de quibus suadeo vos sic habeo.

S. Ignatii Ad
Trallianos

And when this epistle is read among you, cause that it be read also in the church of the Laodiceans.

The broad-backed hippopotamus
Rests on his belly in the mud;
Although he seems so firm to us
He is merely flesh and blood.

Flesh and blood is weak and frail,
Susceptible to nervous shock;
While the True Church can never fail
For it is based upon a rock.

The hippo's feeble steps may err
In compassing material ends,
While the True Church need never stir
To gather in its dividends.

The 'potamus can never reach
The mango on the mango-tree;
But fruits of pomegranate and peach
Refresh the Church from over sea.

At mating time the hippo's voice
Betrays inflexions hoarse and odd,
But every week we hear rejoice
The Church, at being one with God.

The hippopotamus's day
Is passed in sleep; at night he hunts;
God works in a mysterious way—
The Church can sleep and feed at once.

I saw the 'potamus take wing
Ascending from the damp savannas,
And quiring angels round him sing
The praise of God, in loud hosannas.

Blood of the Lamb shall wash him clean
And him shall heavenly arms enfold,
Among the saints he shall be seen
Performing on a harp of gold.

He shall be washed as white as snow,
By all the martyr'd virgins kist,
While the True Church remains below
Wrapt in the old miasmal mist.

Dans le Restaurant

Le garçon délabré qui n'a rien à faire
Que de se gratter les doigts et se pencher sur mon épaule:
 "Dans mon pays il fera temps pluvieux,
 Du vent, du grand soleil, et de la pluie;
 C'est ce qu'on appelle le jour de lessive des gueux."
(Bavard, baveux, à la croupe arrondie,
Je te prie, au moins, ne bave pas dans la soupe).
 "Les saules trempés, et des bourgeons sur les ronces—
 C'est là, dans une averse, qu'on s'abrite.
J'avais sept ans, elle était plus petite.
 Elle était toute mouillée, je lui ai donné des primevères."
Les taches de son gilet montent au chiffre de trentehuit.
 "Je la chatouillais, pour la faire rire.
 J'éprouvais un instant de puissance et de délire."

 Mais alors, vieux lubrique, à cet âge...
"Monsieur, le fait est dur.
 Il est venu, nous peloter, un gros chien;
 Moi j'avais peur, je l'ai quittée à mi-chemin.
 C'est dommage."
  Mais alors, tu as ton vautour!

 Va t'en te décrotter les rides du visage;
Tiens, ma fourchette, décrasse-toi le crâne.
De quel droit payes-tu des expériences comme moi?

Tiens, voilà dix sous, pour la salle-de-bains.

Phlébas, le Phénicien, pendant quinze jours noyé,
Oubliait les cris des mouettes et la houle de Cornouaille,
Et les profits et les pertes, et la cargaison d'étain:
Un courant de sous-mer l'emporta très loin,
Le repassant aux étapes de sa vie antérieure.
Figurez-vous donc, c'était un sort pénible;
Cependant, ce fut jadis un bel homme, de haute taille.

Whispers of Immortality

Webster was much possessed by death
And saw the skull beneath the skin;
And breastless creatures under ground
Leaned backward with a lipless grin.

Daffodil bulbs instead of balls
Stared from the sockets of the eyes!
He knew that thought clings round dead limbs
Tightening its lusts and luxuries.

Donne, I suppose, was such another
Who found no substitute for sense,
To seize and clutch and penetrate;
Expert beyond experience,

He knew the anguish of the marrow
The ague of the skeleton;
No contact possible to flesh
Allayed the fever of the bone.

. . . . .

Grishkin is nice: her Russian eye
Is underlined for emphasis;
Uncorseted, her friendly bust
Gives promise of pneumatic bliss.

The couched Brazilian jaguar
Compels the scampering marmoset
With subtle effluence of cat;
Grishkin has a maisonette;

The sleek Brazilian jaguar
Does not in its arboreal gloom
Distil so rank a feline smell
As Grishkin in a drawing-room.

And even the Abstract Entities
Circumambulate her charm;
But our lot crawls between dry ribs
To keep our metaphysics warm.

Mr. Eliot's Sunday Morning Service

Look, look, master, here comes two religious caterpillars.

The Jew of Malta

Polyphiloprogenitive
The sapient sutlers of the Lord
Drift across the window-panes.
In the beginning was the Word.

In the beginning was the Word.
Superfetation of τὸ ἕν,
And at the mensual turn of time
Produced enervate Origen.

A painter of the Umbrian school
Designed upon a gesso ground
The nimbus of the Baptized God.
The wilderness is cracked and browned

But through the water pale and thin
Still shine the unoffending feet
And there above the painter set
The Father and the Paraclete.

. . . . .

The sable presbyters approach
The avenue of penitence;
The young are red and pustular
Clutching piaculative pence.

Under the penitential gates
Sustained by staring Seraphim
Where the souls of the devout
Burn invisible and dim.

Along the garden-wall the bees
With hairy bellies pass between
The staminate and pistilate,
Blest office of the epicene.

Sweeney shifts from ham to ham
Stirring the water in his bath.
The masters of the subtle schools
Are controversial, polymath.

Sweeney among the Nightingales

ὤμοι, πέπληγμαι καιρίαν πληγὴν ἔσω

Apeneck Sweeney spreads his knees
Letting his arms hang down to laugh,
The zebra stripes along his jaw
Swelling to maculate giraffe.

The circles of the stormy moon
Slide westward toward the River Plate,
Death and the Raven drift above
And Sweeney guards the hornèd gate.

Gloomy Orion and the Dog
Are veiled; and hushed the shrunken seas;
The person in the Spanish cape
Tries to sit on Sweeney's knees

Slips and pulls the table cloth
Overturns a coffee-cup,
Reorganised upon the floor
She yawns and draws a stocking up;

The silent man in mocha brown
Sprawls at the window-sill and gapes;
The waiter brings in oranges
Bananas figs and hothouse grapes;

The silent vertebrate in brown
Contracts and concentrates, withdraws;
Rachel *née* Rabinovitch
Tears at the grapes with murderous paws;

She and the lady in the cape
Are suspect, thought to be in league;
Therefore the man with heavy eyes
Declines the gambit, shows fatigue,

Leaves the room and reappears
Outside the window, leaning in,
Branches of wistaria
Circumscribe a golden grin;

The host with someone indistinct
Converses at the door apart,
The nightingales are singing near
The Convent of the Sacred Heart,

And sang within the bloody wood
When Agamemnon cried aloud,
And let their liquid siftings fall
To stain the stiff dishonoured shroud.

The Waste Land [1]

1. Not only the title, but the plan and a good deal of the incidental symbolism of the poem were suggested by Miss Jessie L. Weston's book on the Grail legend: *From Ritual to Romance* (Macmillan). Indeed, so deeply am I indebted, Miss Weston's book will elucidate the difficulties of the poem much better than my notes can do; and I recommend it (apart from the great interest of the book itself) to any who think such elucidation of the poem worth the trouble. To another work of anthropology I am indebted in general, one which has influenced our generation profoundly; I mean *The Golden Bough;* I have used especially the two volumes *Adonis, Attis, Osiris.* Anyone who is acquainted with these works will immediately recognize in the poem certain references to vegetation ceremonies.

Nam Sibyllam quidem Cumis ego ipse oculis meis vidi in ampulla pendere, et cum illi pueri dicerent: Σίβυλλα τί θέλεις· *respondebat illa:* ἀποθανεῖν θέλω.

I. The Burial of the Dead

April is the cruellest month, breeding
Lilacs out of the dead land, mixing
Memory and desire, stirring
Dull roots with spring rain.
Winter kept us warm, covering
Earth in forgetful snow, feeding
A little life with dried tubers.
Summer surprised us, coming over the Starnbergersee
With a shower of rain; we stopped in the colonnade,
And went on in sunlight, into the Hofgarten,
And drank coffee, and talked for an hour.
Bin gar keine Russin, stamm' aus Litauen, echt deutsch.
And when we were children, staying at the archduke's,
My cousin's, he took me out on a sled,
And I was frightened. He said, Marie,
Marie, hold on tight. And down we went.
In the mountains, there you feel free.
I read, much of the night, and go south in the winter.

What are the roots that clutch, what branches grow
Out of this stony rubbish? Son of man,[1]
You cannot say, or guess, for you know only
A heap of broken images, where the sun beats,

---

1. Cf. Ezekiel 2:7.

And the dead tree gives no shelter, the cricket no relief,[1]
And the dry stone no sound of water. Only
There is shadow under this red rock,
(Come in under the shadow of this red rock),
And I will show you something different from either
Your shadow at morning striding behind you
Or your shadow at evening rising to meet you;
I will show you fear in a handful of dust.

Frisch weht der Wind[2]
Der Heimat zu.
Mein Irisch Kind,
Wo weilest du?

'You gave me hyacinths first a year ago;
'They called me the hyacinth girl.'
—Yet when we came back, late, from the Hyacinth garden,
Your arms full, and your hair wet, I could not
Speak, and my eyes failed, I was neither
Living nor dead, and I knew nothing,
Looking into the heart of light, the silence.
Od' und leer das Meer.[3]

Madame Sosostris, famous clairvoyante,
Had a bad cold, nevertheless
Is known to be the wisest woman in Europe,
With a wicked pack of cards. Here, said she,[4]

---

1. Cf. Ecclesiastes 12:5.
2. V. *Tristan und Isolde*, i, verses 5–8.
3. Id. iii, verse 24.
4. I am not familiar with the exact constitution of the Tarot pack of cards, from which I have obviously departed to suit my own convenience. The Hanged Man, a member of the traditional pack, fits my purpose in two ways: because he is associated in my mind with the Hanged God of Frazer, and because I associate him with the hooded figure in the passage of the disciples to Emmaus in Part V.

Is your card, the drowned Phoenician Sailor,
(Those are pearls that were his eyes. Look!)
Here is Belladonna, the Lady of the Rocks,
The lady of situations.
Here is the man with three staves, and here the Wheel,
And here is the one-eyed merchant, and this card,
Which is blank, is something he carries on his back,
Which I am forbidden to see. I do not find
The Hanged Man. Fear death by water.
I see crowds of people, walking round in a ring.
Thank you. If you see dear Mrs. Equitone,
Tell her I bring the horoscope myself:
One must be so careful these days.

Unreal City,[1]
Under the brown fog of a winter dawn,
A crowd flowed over London Bridge, so many,
I had not thought death had undone so many.[2]
Sighs, short and infrequent, were exhaled,[3]
And each man fixed his eyes before his feet.
Flowed up the hill and down King William Street,
To where Saint Mary Woolnoth kept the hours

The Phoenician Sailor and the Merchant appear later; also the 'crowds of people,' and Death by Water is executed in Part IV. The Man with Three Staves (an authentic member of the Tarot pack) I associate, quite arbitrarily, with the Fisher King himself.

1. Cf. Baudelaire:
Fourmillante cité, cité pleine de rêves,
Où le spectre en plein jour raccroche le passant.

2. Cf. *Inferno,* iii. 55–7:
si lunga tratta
di gente, ch'io non avrei mai creduto
che morte tanta n'avesse disfatta.

3. Cf. *Inferno,* iv. 25–27:
Quivi, secondo che per ascoltare,
non avea pianto, ma' che di sospiri,
che l'aura eterna facevan tremare.

With a dead sound on the final stroke of nine.[1]
There I saw one I knew, and stopped him, crying 'Stetson!
'You who were with me in the ships at Mylae!
'That corpse you planted last year in your garden,
'Has it begun to sprout? Will it bloom this year?
'Or has the sudden frost disturbed its bed?
'Oh keep the Dog far hence, that's friend to men,[2]
'Or with his nails he'll dig it up again!
'You! hypocrite lecteur!—mon semblable,—mon frère!'[3]

---

1. A phenomenon which I have often noticed.
2. Cf. the Dirge in Webster's *White Devil.*
3. V. Baudelaire, Preface to *Fleurs du Mal.*

II. A Game of Chess

The Chair she sat in, like a burnished throne,[1]
Glowed on the marble, where the glass
Held up by standards wrought with fruited vines
From which a golden Cupidon peeped out
(Another hid his eyes behind his wing)
Doubled the flames of sevenbranched candelabra
Reflecting light upon the table as
The glitter of her jewels rose to meet it,
From satin cases poured in rich profusion;
In vials of ivory and coloured glass
Unstoppered, lurked her strange synthetic perfumes,
Unguent, powdered, or liquid—troubled, confused
And drowned the sense in odours; stirred by the air
That freshened from the window, these ascended
In fattening the prolonged candle-flames,
Flung their smoke into the laquearia,[2]
Stirring the pattern on the coffered ceiling.
Huge sea-wood fed with copper
Burned green and orange, framed by the coloured stone,
In which sad light a carvèd dolphin swam.
Above the antique mantel was displayed

---

1. Cf. *Antony and Cleopatra*, II. ii. 190.
2. Laquearia. V. *Aeneid*, I. 726:
dependent lychni laquearibus aureis incensi, et noctem flammis funalia vincunt.

As though a window gave upon the sylvan scene[1]
The change of Philomel, by the barbarous king[2]
So rudely forced; yet there the nightingale[3]
Filled all the desert with inviolable voice
And still she cried, and still the world pursues,
'Jug Jug' to dirty ears.
And other withered stumps of time
Were told upon the walls; staring forms
Leaned out, leaning, hushing the room enclosed.
Footsteps shuffled on the stair.
Under the firelight, under the brush, her hair
Spread out in fiery points
Glowed into words, then would be savagely still.

'My nerves are bad to-night. Yes, bad. Stay with me.
'Speak to me. Why do you never speak. Speak.
'What are you thinking of? What thinking? What?
'I never know what you are thinking. Think.'

I think we are in rats' alley[4]
Where the dead men lost their bones.

'What is that noise?'
The wind under the door.[5]
'What is that noise now? What is the wind doing?'
Nothing again nothing.
'Do
'You know nothing? Do you see nothing? Do you remember
'Nothing?'

---

1. Sylvan scene. V. Milton, *Paradise Lost*, iv. 140.
2. V. Ovid, *Metamorphoses*, vi, Philomela.
3. Cf. Part III,1. 204.
4. Cf. Part III,1. 195.
5. Cf. Webster: 'Is the wind in that door still?'

I remember
Those are pearls that were his eyes.
'Are you alive, or not? Is there nothing in your head?'[1]
But
O O O O that Shakespeherian Rag—
It's so elegant
So intelligent
'What shall I do now? What shall I do?'
'I shall rush out as I am, and walk the street
'With my hair down, so. What shall we do to-morrow?
'What shall we ever do?'
The hot water at ten.
And if it rains, a closed car at four.
And we shall play a game of chess,
Pressing lidless eyes and waiting for a knock upon the door.[2]

When Lil's husband got demobbed, I said—
I didn't mince my words, I said to her myself,
HURRY UP PLEASE IT'S TIME
Now Albert's coming back, make yourself a bit smart.
He'll want to know what you done with that money he gave
you
To get yourself some teeth. He did, I was there.
You have them all out, Lil, and get a nice set,
He said, I swear, I can't bear to look at you.
And no more can't I, I said, and think of poor Albert,
He's been in the army four years, he wants a good time,
And if you don't give it him, there's others will, I said.
Oh is there, she said. Something o' that, I said.

---

1. Cf. Part I, l. 37, 48.
2. Cf. the game of chess in Middleton's *Women beware Women*.

Then I'll know who to thank, she said, and give me a straight look.
HURRY UP PLEASE IT'S TIME
If you don't like it you can get on with it, I said.
Others can pick and choose if you can't.
But if Albert makes off, it won't be for lack of telling.
You ought to be ashamed, I said, to look so antique.
(And her only thirty-one.)
I can't help it, she said, pulling a long face,
It's them pills I took, to bring it off, she said.
(She's had five already, and nearly died of young George.)
The chemist said it would be alright, but I've never been the same.
You *are* a proper fool, I said.
Well, if Albert won't leave you alone, there it is, I said,
What you get married for if you don't want children?
HURRY UP PLEASE IT'S TIME
Well, that Sunday Albert was home, they had a hot gammon,
And they asked me in to dinner, to get the beauty of it hot—
HURRY UP PLEASE IT'S TIME
HURRY UP PLEASE IT'S TIME
Goonight Bill. Goonight Lou. Goonight May. Goonight.
Ta ta. Goonight. Goonight.
Good night, ladies, good night, sweet ladies, good night, good night.

III. The Fire Sermon

The river's tent is broken: the last fingers of leaf
Clutch and sink into the wet bank. The wind
Crosses the brown land, unheard. The nymphs are departed.
Sweet Thames, run softly, till I end my song.[1]
The river bears no empty bottles, sandwich papers,
Silk handkerchiefs, cardboard boxes, cigarette ends
Or other testimony of summer nights. The nymphs are
departed.
And their friends, the loitering heirs of city directors;
Departed, have left no addresses.
By the waters of Leman I sat down and wept . . .
Sweet Thames, run softly till I end my song,
Sweet Thames, run softly, for I speak not loud or long.
But at my back in a cold blast I hear
The rattle of the bones, and chuckle spread from ear to ear.
A rat crept softly through the vegetation
Dragging its slimy belly on the bank
While I was fishing in the dull canal
On a winter evening round behind the gashouse
Musing upon the king my brother's wreck
And on the king my father's death before him.[2]
White bodies naked on the low damp ground

---

1. V. Spenser, *Prothalamion.*
2. Cf. *The Tempest,* I. ii.

And bones cast in a little low dry garret,
Rattled by the rat's foot only, year to year.
But at my back from time to time I hear[1]
The sound of horns and motors, which shall bring[2]
Sweeney to Mrs. Porter in the spring.
O the moon shone bright on Mrs. Porter[3]
And on her daughter
They wash their feet in soda water
Et O ces voix d'enfants, chantant dans la coupole![4]

Twit twit twit
Jug jug jug jug jug jug
So rudely forc'd.
Tereu

Unreal City
Under the brown fog of a winter noon
Mr. Eugenides, the Smyrna merchant
Unshaven, with a pocket full of currants[5]
C.i.f. London: documents at sight,
Asked me in demotic French
To luncheon at the Cannon Street Hotel
Followed by a weekend at the Metropole.

At the violet hour, when the eyes and back

---

1. Cf. Marvell, "To His Coy Mistress."

2. Cf. Day, *Parliament of Bees:*

When of the sudden, listening, you shall hear,
A noise of horns and hunting, which shall bring
Actaeon to Diana in the spring,
Where all shall see her naked skin . . .'

3. I do not know the origin of the ballad from which these lines are taken: it was reported to me from Sydney, Australia.

4. V. Verlaine, *Parsifal.*

5. The currants were quoted at a price 'carriage and insurance free to London'; and the Bill of Lading, etc., were to be handed to the buyer upon payment of the sight draft.

Turn upward from the desk, when the human engine waits
Like a taxi throbbing waiting,
I Tiresias, though blind, throbbing between two lives,[1]
Old man with wrinkled female breasts, can see
At the violet hour, the evening hour that strives
Homeward, and brings the sailor home from sea,[2]
The typist home at teatime, clears her breakfast, lights
Her stove, and lays out food in tins.
Out of the window perilously spread
Her drying combinations touched by the sun's last rays,
On the divan are piled (at night her bed)
Stockings, slippers, camisoles, and stays.
I Tiresias, old man with wrinkled dugs
Perceived the scene, and foretold the rest—

---

1. Tiresias, although a mere spectator and not indeed a 'character,' is yet the most important personage in the poem, uniting all the rest. Just as the one-eyed merchant, seller of currants, melts into the Phoenician Sailor, and the latter is not wholly distinct from Ferdinand Prince of Naples, so all the women are one woman, and the two sexes meet in Tiresias. What Tiresias sees, in fact, is the substance of the poem. The whole passage from Ovid is of great anthropological interest:

. . . Cum Iunone iocos et 'maior vestra profecto est
Quam, quae contingit maribus,' dixisse, 'voluptas.'
Illa negat; placuit quae sit sententia docti
Quaerere Tiresiae: venus huic erat utraque nota.
Nam duo magnorum viridi coeuntia silva
Corpora serpentum baculi violaverat ictu
Deque viro factus, mirabile, femina septem
Egerat autumnos; octavo rursus eosdem
Vidit et 'est vestrae si tanta potentia plagae,'
Dixit 'ut auctoris sortem in contraria mutet,
Nunc quoque vos feriam!' percussis anguibus isdem
Forma prior rediit genetivaque venit imago.
Arbiter hic igitur sumptus de lite iocosa
Dicta Iovis firmat; gravius Saturnia iusto
Nec pro materia fertur doluisse suique
Iudicis aeterna damnavit lumina nocte,
At pater omnipotens (neque enim licet inrita cuiquam
Facta dei fecisse deo) pro lumine adempto
Scire futura dedit poenamque levavit honore.

2. This may not appear as exact as Sappho's lines, but I had in mind the 'longshore' or 'dory' fisherman, who returns at nightfall.

I too awaited the expected guest.
He, the young man carbuncular, arrives,
A small house agent's clerk, with one bold stare,
One of the low on whom assurance sits
As a silk hat on a Bradford millionaire.
The time is now propitious, as he guesses,
The meal is ended, she is bored and tired,
Endeavours to engage her in caresses
Which still are unreproved, if undesired.
Flushed and decided, he assaults at once;
Exploring hands encounter no defence;
His vanity requires no response,
And makes a welcome of indifference.
(And I Tiresias have foresuffered all
Enacted on this same divan or bed;
I who have sat by Thebes below the wall
And walked among the lowest of the dead.)
Bestows one final patronising kiss,
And gropes his way, finding the stairs unlit . . .

She turns and looks a moment in the glass,
Hardly aware of her departed lover;
Her brain allows one half-formed thought to pass:
'Well now that's done: and I'm glad it's over.'
When lovely woman stoops to folly and[1]
Paces about her room again, alone,
She smoothes her hair with automatic hand,
And puts a record on the gramophone.

'This music crept by me upon the waters'[2]
And along the Strand, up Queen Victoria Street.

---

1. V. Goldsmith, the song in *The Vicar of Wakefield.*
2. V. *The Tempest,* as above.

O City city, I can sometimes hear
Beside a public bar in Lower Thames Street,
The pleasant whining of a mandoline
And a clatter and a chatter from within
Where fishmen lounge at noon: where the walls
Of Magnus Martyr hold[1]
Inexplicable splendour of Ionian white and gold.

The river sweats[2]
Oil and tar
The barges drift
With the turning tide
Red sails
Wide
To leeward, swing on the heavy spar.
The barges wash
Drifting logs
Down Greenwich reach
Past the Isle of Dogs.
Weialala leia
Wallala leialala

Elizabeth and Leicester[3]
Beating oars
The stern was formed
A gilded shell

---

1. The interior of St. Magnus Martyr is to my mind one of the finest among Wren's interiors. See *The Proposed Demolition of Nineteen City Churches* (P. S. King & Son, Ltd.).

2. The Song of the (three) Thames-daughters begins here. From line 292 to 306 inclusive they speak in turn. V. Götterdammerung, III. i: The Rhine-daughters.

3. V. Froude, Elizabeth, vol. I, ch. iv, letter of De Quadra to Philip of Spain:
In the afternoon we were in a barge, watching the games on the river. (The queen) was alone with Lord Robert and myself on the poop, when they began to talk nonsense, and went so far that Lord Robert at last said, as I was on the spot there was no reason why they should not be married if the queen pleased.

Red and gold
The brisk swell
Rippled both shores
Southwest wind
Carried down stream
The peal of bells
White towers
Weialala leia
Wallala leialala

'Trams and dusty trees.
Highbury bore me. Richmond and Kew[1]
Undid me. By Richmond I raised my knees
Supine on the floor of a narrow canoe.'

'My feet are at Moorgate, and my heart
Under my feet. After the event
He wept. He promised "a new start."
I made no comment. What should I resent?'

'On Margate Sands.
I can connect
Nothing with nothing.
The broken fingernails of dirty hands.
My people humble people who expect
Nothing.'
la la

To Carthage then I came[2]

---

1. Cf. *Purgatorio,* V. 133:
'Ricorditi di me, che son la Pia;
Siena mi fe,' disfecemi Maremma.'

2. V. St. Augustine's *Confessions:* 'to Carthage then I came, where a cauldron of unholy loves sang all about mine ears.'

Burning burning burning burning[1]
O Lord Thou pluckest me out[2]
O Lord Thou pluckest

burning

---

1. The complete text of the Buddha's Fire Sermon (which corresponds in importance to the Sermon on the Mount) from which these words are taken, will be found translated in the late Henry Clarke Warren's *Buddhism in Translation* (Harvard Oriental Series). Mr. Warren was one of the great pioneers of Buddhist studies in the Occident.

2. From St. Augustine's *Confessions again.* The collocation of these two representatives of eastern and western asceticism, as the culmination of this part of the poem, is not an accident.

IV. Death by Water

Phlebas the Phoenician, a fortnight dead,
Forgot the cry of gulls, and the deep seas swell
And the profit and loss.
                                                    A current under sea
Picked his bones in whispers. As he rose and fell
He passed the stages of his age and youth
Entering the whirlpool.
                                                    Gentile or Jew
O you who turn the wheel and look to windward,
Consider Phlebas, who was once handsome and tall as you.

V. What the Thunder Said[1]

After the torchlight red on sweaty faces
After the frosty silence in the gardens
After the agony in stony places
The shouting and the crying
Prison and palace and reverberation
Of thunder of spring over distant mountains
He who was living is now dead
We who were living are now dying
With a little patience

Here is no water but only rock
Rock and no water and the sandy road
The road winding above among the mountains
Which are mountains of rock without water
If there were water we should stop and drink
Amongst the rock one cannot stop or think
Sweat is dry and feet are in the sand
If there were only water amongst the rock
Dead mountain mouth of carious teeth that cannot spit
Here one can neither stand nor lie nor sit
There is not even silence in the mountains
But dry sterile thunder without rain

---

1. In the first part of Part V three themes are employed: the journey to Emmaus, the approach to the Chapel Perilous (see Miss Weston's book), and the present decay of eastern Europe.

There is not even solitude in the mountains
But red sullen faces sneer and snarl
From doors of mudcracked houses
                                        If there were water
    And no rock
    If there were rock
    And also water
    And water
    A spring
    A pool among the rock
    If there were the sound of water only
    Not the cicada
    And dry grass singing
    But sound of water over a rock
    Where the hermit-thrush sings in the pine trees
    Drip drop drip drop drop drop drop[1]
    But there is no water

    Who is the third who walks always beside you?
When I count, there are only you and I together[2]
But when I look ahead up the white road
There is always another one walking beside you
Gliding wrapt in a brown mantle, hooded
I do not know whether a man or a woman
—But who is that on the other side of you?

---

1. This is Turdus aonalaschkae pallasii, the hermit-thrush which I have heard in Quebec County. Chapman says (*Handbook of Birds in Eastern North America*) 'it is most at home in secluded woodland and thickety retreats. . . . Its notes are not remarkable for variety or volume, but in purity and sweetness of tone and exquisite modulation they are unequalled.' Its 'water-dripping song' is justly celebrated.

2. The following lines were stimulated by the account of one of the Antarctic expeditions (I forget which, but I think one of Shackleton's): it was related that the party of explorers, at the extremity of their strength, had the constant delusion that there was one more member than could actually be counted.

What is that sound high in the air
Murmur of maternal lamentation[1]
Who are those hooded hordes swarming
Over endless plains, stumbling in cracked earth
Ringed by the flat horizon only
What is the city over the mountains
Cracks and reforms and bursts in the violet air
Falling towers
Jerusalem Athens Alexandria
Vienna London
Unreal
A woman drew her long black hair out tight
And fiddled whisper music on those strings
And bats with baby faces in the violet light
Whistled, and beat their wings
And crawled head downward down a blackened wall
And upside down in air were towers
Tolling reminiscent bells, that kept the hours
And voices singing out of empty cisterns and exhausted
wells.

In this decayed hole among the mountains
In the faint moonlight, the grass is singing
Over the tumbled graves, about the chapel
There is the empty chapel, only the wind's home.
It has no windows, and the door swings,
Dry bones can harm no one.
Only a cock stood on the rooftree
Co co rico co co rico

---

1. This line and the following nine lines, cf. Hermann Hesse, *Blick ins Chaos:* Schon ist halb Europa, schon ist zumindest der halbe Osten Europas auf dem Wege zum Chaos, fährt betrunken im heiligen Wahn am Abgrund entlang und singt dazu, singt betrunken und hymnisch wie Dmitri Karamasoff sang. Ueber diese Lieder lacht der Bürger beleidigt, der Heilige und Seher hört sie mit Tränen.

In a flash of lightning. Then a damp gust
Bringing rain

Ganga was sunken, and the limp leaves
Waited for rain, while the black clouds
Gathered far distant, over Himavant.
The jungle crouched, humped in silence.
Then spoke the thunder
DA
Datta: what have we given?[1]
My friend, blood shaking my heart
The awful daring of a moment's surrender
Which an age of prudence can never retract
By this, and this only, we have existed
Which is not to be found in our obituaries
Or in memories draped by the beneficent spider[2]
Or under seals broken by the lean solicitor
In our empty rooms
DA
Dayadhvam: I have heard the key[3]
Turn in the door once and turn once only
We think of the key, each in his prison

---

1. 'Datta, dayadhvam, damyata' (Give, sympathize, control). The fable of the meaning of the Thunder is found in the Brihadaranyaka—Upanishad, 5, 1. A translation is found in Deussen's Sechzig *Upanishads des Veda,* p. 489.

2. Cf. Webster, *The White Devil,* V, vi:

. . . they'll remarry
Ere the worm pierce your winding-sheet, ere the spider
Make a thin curtain for your epitaphs.

3. Cf. *Inferno,* xxxiii. 46:

ed io sentii chiavar l'uscio di sotto
all'orribile torre.

Also F. H. Bradley, *Appearance and Reality,* p. 346:

My external sensations are no less private to myself than are my thoughts or my feelings. In either case my experience falls within my own circle, a circle closed on the outside; and, with all its elements alike, every sphere is opaque to the others which surround it. . . . In brief, regarded as an existence which appears in a soul, the whole world for each is peculiar and private to that soul.

Thinking of the key, each confirms a prison
Only at nightfall, aetherial rumours
Revive for a moment a broken Coriolanus
DA
Damyata: The boat responded
Gaily, to the hand expert with sail and oar
The sea was calm, your heart would have responded
Gaily, when invited, beating obedient
To controlling hands

I sat upon the shore
Fishing, with the arid plain behind me[1]
Shall I at least set my lands in order?
London Bridge is falling down falling down falling down
Poi s'ascose nel foco che gli affina[2]
Quando fiam uti chelidon—O swallow swallow[3]
Le Prince d' Aquitaine à la tour abolie[4]
These fragments I have shored against my ruins
Why then Ile fit you. Hieronymo's mad againe.[5]
Datta. Dayadhvam. Damyata.
Shantih shantih shantih[6]

---

1. V. Weston, *From Ritual to Romance;* chapter on the Fisher King.
2. V. *Purgatorio,* xxvi. 148.
'Ara vos prec per aquella valor
'que vos guida al som de l'escalina,
'sovegna vos a temps de ma dolor.'
Poi s'ascose nel foco che gli affina.
3. V. *Pervigilium Veneris.* Cf. Philomela in Parts II and III.
4. V. Gerard de Nerval, *Sonnet El Desdichado.*
5. V. Kyd's *Spanish Tragedy.*
6. Shantih. Repeated as here, a formal ending to an Upanishad. 'The Peace which passeth understanding' is a feeble translation of the conduct of this word.

Eeldrop and Appleplex[1]

1. This story, which appeared in *The Little Review* literary magazine in 1917, was the adult Eliot's only piece of published fiction.

I

Eeldrop and Appleplex rented two small rooms in a disreputable part of town. Here they sometimes came at nightfall, here they sometimes slept, and after they had slept, they cooked oatmeal and departed in the morning for destinations unknown to each other. They sometimes slept, more often they talked, or looked out of the window.

They had chosen the rooms and the neighborhood with great care. There are evil neighborhoods of noise and evil neighborhoods of silence, and Eeldrop and Appleplex preferred the latter, as being the more evil. It was a shady street, its windows were heavily curtained; and over it hung the cloud of a respectability which has something to conceal. Yet it had the advantage of more riotous neighborhoods near by, and Eeldrop and Appleplex commanded from their windows the entrance of a police station across the way. This alone possessed an irresistible appeal in their eyes. From time to time the silence of the street was broken; whenever a malefactor was apprehended, a wave of excitement curled into the street and broke upon the doors of the police station. Then the inhabitants of the street would linger in dressing-gowns, upon their doorsteps: then alien visitors would linger in the street, in caps; long after the centre of misery had been engulphed in his cell. Then Eeldrop and Appleplex would break off their discourse, and rush out to mingle with the mob. Each pursued his own line of enquiry. Appleplex, who had the gift of an extraordinary address with the lower classes of both sexes, questioned the onlookers, and usually extracted full and inconsistent histories: Eeldrop preserved a more passive demeanor, listened to the conversation of the people among themselves, registered in his mind their oaths, their redundance of phrase, their various manners of spitting, and the cries of the victim from the hall of justice within. When the crowd dispersed, Eeldrop and Appleplex returned to their rooms: Appleplex entered the results of his inquiries into large notebooks, filed according to the nature of the case, from A (adultery) to Y (yeggmen). Eeldrop smoked reflectively. It may be added that Eeldrop was a sceptic, with a taste for mysticism, and Appleplex a materialist with a leaning toward scepticism; that Eeldrop was learned in theology, and that Appleplex studied the physical and biological sciences.

There was a common motive which led Eeldrop and Appleplex thus to separate themselves from time to time, from the fields of their daily employments and their ordinarily social activities. Both were endeavoring to escape not the commonplace, respectable or even the domestic, but the too well pigeonholed, too taken-for-granted, too highly systematized areas, and,—in the language of those whom they sought to avoid—they wished "to apprehend the human soul in its concrete individuality."

"Why," said Eeldrop, "was that fat Spaniard, who sat at the table with us this evening, and listened to our conversation with occasional curiosity, why was he himself for a moment an object of interest to us? He wore his napkin tucked into his chin, he made unpleasant noises while eating, and while not eating, his way of crumbling bread between fat fingers made me extremely nervous: he wore a waistcoat cafe au lait, and black boots with brown tops. He was oppressively gross and vulgar; he belonged to a type, he could easily be classified in any town of provincial Spain. Yet under the circumstances—when we had been discussing marriage, and he suddenly leaned forward and exclaimed: 'I was married once myself'—we were able to detach him from his classification and regard him for a moment as an unique being, a soul, however insignificant, with a history of its own, once for all. It is these moments which we prize, and which alone are revealing. For any vital truth is incapable of being applied to another case: the essential is unique. Perhaps that is why it is so neglected: because it is useless. What we learned about that Spaniard is incapable of being applied to any other Spaniard, or even recalled in words. With the decline of orthodox theology and its admirable theory of the soul, the unique importance of events has vanished. A man is only important as he is classed. Hence there is no tragedy, or no appreciation of tragedy, which is the same thing. We had been talking of young Bistwick, who three months ago married his mother's housemaid and now is aware of the fact. Who appreciates the truth of the matter? Not the relatives, for they are only moved by affection, by regard for Bistwick's interests, and chiefly by their collective feeling of family disgrace. Not the generous minded and thoughtful outsider, who regards it merely as evidence for the necessity of divorce law reform. Bistwick is classed among the unhappily married. But what Bistwick feels when he wakes up in the morning, which is the great important fact, no detached outsider conceives. The awful importance of the ruin of a life is overlooked. Men are only allowed to be happy or miserable in classes. In Gopsum Street a man murders his mistress. The important fact is that for the man the act is eternal, and that for the brief space he has to live, he is already dead. He is already in a different world from ours. He has crossed the frontier. The important fact is that something is done which can not be undone—a possibility which none of us realize until we face it ourselves. For the man's neighbors the important fact is what the man killed her with? And at precisely what time? And who found the body? For the 'enlightened public' the case is merely evidence for the Drink question, or Unemployment, or some other category of things to be reformed. But the mediaeval world, insisting on the eternity of punishment, expressed something nearer the truth."

"What you say," replied Appleplex, "commands my measured adherence. I should think, in the case of the Spaniard, and in the many other interesting cases which have come under our attention at the door of the police station, what we grasp in that moment of pure observation on which we pride ourselves, is not alien to the principle of classification, but deeper. We could, if we liked, make excellent comment upon the nature of provincial Spaniards, or of destitution (as misery is called by the philanthropists), or on homes for working girls. But such is not our intention. We aim at experience in the particular centres in which alone it is evil. We avoid classification. We do not deny it. But when a man is classified something is lost. The majority of mankind live on paper currency: they use terms which are merely good for so much reality, they never see actual coinage."

"I should go even further than that," said Eeldrop. "The majority not only have no language to express anything save generalized man; they are for the most part unaware of themselves as anything but generalized men. They are first of all government officials, or pillars of the church, or trade unionists, or poets, or unemployed; this cataloguing is not only satisfactory to other people for practical purposes, it is sufficient to themselves for their 'life of the spirit.' Many are not quite real at any moment. When Wolstrip married, I am sure he said to himself: 'Now I am consummating the union of two of the best families in Philadelphia.'"

"The question is," said Appleplex, "what is to be our philosophy. This must be settled at once. Mrs. Howexden recommends me to read Bergson. He writes very entertainingly on the structure of the eye of the frog."

"Not at all," interrupted his friend. "Our philosophy is quite irrelevant. The essential is, that our philosophy should spring from our point of view and not return upon itself to explain our point of view. A philosophy about intuition is somewhat less likely to be intuitive than any other. We must avoid having a platform."

"But at least," said Appleplex, "we are . . ."

"Individualists. No!! nor anti-intellectualists. These also are labels. The 'individualist' is a member of a mob as fully as any other man: and the mob of individualists is the most unpleasing, because it has the least character. Nietzsche was a mob-man, just as Bergson is an intellectualist. We cannot escape the label, but let it be one which carries no distinction, and arouses no self-consciousness. Sufficient that we should find simple labels, and not further exploit them. I am, I confess to you, in private life, a bank-clerk. . . ."

"And should, according to your own view, have a wife, three children, and a vegetable garden in a suburb," said Appleplex.

"Such is precisely the case," returned Eeldrop, "but I had not thought it necessary to mention this biographical detail. As it is Saturday night, I shall return to my suburb. Tomorrow will be spent in that garden. . . ."

"I shall pay my call on Mrs. Howexden," murmured Appleplex.

II

The suburban evening was grey and yellow on Sunday; the gardens of the small houses to left and right were rank with ivy and tall grass and lilac bushes; the tropical South London verdure was dusty above and mouldy below; the tepid air swarmed with flies. Eeldrop, at the window, welcomed the smoky smell of lilac, the gramaphones, the choir of the Baptist chapel, and the sight of three small girls playing cards on the steps of the police station.

"On such a night as this," said Eeldrop, "I often think of Scheherazade, and wonder what has become of her."

Appleplex rose without speaking and turned to the files which contained the documents for his "Survey of Contemporary Society." He removed the file marked *London* from between the files *Barcelona* and *Boston* where it had been misplaced, and turned over the papers rapidly. "The lady you mention," he rejoined at last, "whom I have listed not under S. but as Edith, alias Scheherazade, has left but few evidences in my possession. Here is an old laundry account which she left for you to pay, a cheque drawn by her and marked 'R/D,' a letter from her mother in Honolulu (on ruled paper), a poem written on a restaurant bill—'To Atthis'—and a letter by herself, on Lady Equistep's best notepaper, containing some damaging but entertaining information about Lady Equistep. Then there are my own few observations on two sheets of foolscap."

"Edith," murmured Eeldrop, who had not been attending to this catalogue, "I wonder what has become of her. 'Not pleasure, but fulness of life . . . to burn ever with a hard gem-like flame,' those were her words. What curiosity and passion for experience! Perhaps that flame has burnt itself out by now."

"You ought to inform yourself better," said Appleplex severely, "Edith dines sometimes with Mrs. Howexden, who tells me that her passion for experience has taken her to a Russian pianist in Bayswater. She is also said to be present often at the Anarchist Tea Rooms, and can usually be found in the evening at the Cafe de l'Orangerie."

"Well," replied Eeldrop, "I confess that I prefer to wonder what has become of her. I do not like to think of her future. Scheherazade grown old! I see her grown very plump, full-bosomed, with blond hair, living in a small flat with a maid, walking in the Park with a Pekinese, motoring with a Jewish stock-broker. With a fierce appetite for food and drink, when all other appetite is gone, all other appetite gone except the insatiable increasing appetite of vanity; rolling on two wide legs, rolling in motorcars, rolling toward a diabetic end in a seaside watering place."

"Just now you saw that bright flame burning itself out," said Appleplex, "now you see it guttering thickly, which proves that your vision was founded on imagination, not on feeling. And the passion for experience—have you remained so impregnably Pre-Raphaelite as to believe in that? What real person, with the genuine resources of instinct, has ever believed in the passion for experience? The passion for experience is a criticism of the sincere, a creed only of the histrionic. The passionate person is passionate about this or that, perhaps about the least significant things, but not about experience. But Marius, des Esseintes, Edith . . ."

"But consider," said Eeldrop, attentive only to the facts of Edith's history, and perhaps missing the point of Appleplex's remarks, "her unusual career. The daughter of a piano tuner in Honolulu, she secured a scholarship at the University of California, where she graduated with Honors in Social Ethics. She then married a celebrated billiard professional in San Francisco, after an acquaintance of twelve hours, lived with him for two days, joined a musical comedy chorus, and was divorced in Nevada. She turned up several years later in Paris and was known to all the Americans and English at the Cafe du Dome as Mrs. Short. She reappeared in London as Mrs. Griffiths, published a small volume of verse, and was accepted in several circles known to us. And now, as I still insist, she has disappeared from society altogether."

"The memory of Scheherazade," said Appleplex, "is to me that of Bird's custard and prunes in a Bloomsbury boarding house. It is not my intention to represent Edith as merely disreputable. Neither is she a tragic figure. I want to know why she misses. I cannot altogether analyse her 'into a combination of known elements' but I fail to touch anything definitely unanalysable.

"Is Edith, in spite of her romantic past, pursuing steadily some hidden purpose of her own? Are her migrations and eccentricities the sign of some unguessed consistency? I find in her a quantity of shrewd observation, an excellent fund of criticism, but I cannot connect them into any peculiar vision. Her sarcasm at the expense of her friends is delightful, but I doubt whether it is more than an attempt to mould herself from outside, by the impact of hostilities, to emphasise her isolation. Everyone says of her, 'How perfectly impenetrable!' I suspect that within there is only the confusion of a dusty garret."

"I test people," said Eeldrop, "by the way in which I imagine them as waking up in the morning. I am not drawing upon memory when I imagine Edith waking to a room strewn with clothes, papers, cosmetics, letters and a few books, the smell of Violettes de Parme and stale tobacco. The sunlight beating in through broken blinds, and broken blinds keeping out the sun until Edith can compel herself to attend to another day. Yet the vision does not give me much pain. I think of her as an artist without the slightest artistic power."

"The artistic temperament—" began Appleplex.

"No, not that." Eeldrop snatched away the opportunity. "I mean that what holds the artist together is the work which he does; separate him from his work and he either disintegrates or solidifies. There is no interest in the artist apart from his work. And there are, as you said, those people who provide material for the artist. Now Edith's poem 'To Atthis' proves beyond the shadow of a doubt that she is not an artist. On the other hand I have often thought of her, as I thought this evening, as presenting possibilities for poetic purposes. But the people who can be material for art must have in them something unconscious, something which they do not fully realise or understand. Edith, in spite of what is called her impenetrable mask, presents herself too well.. I cannot use her; she uses herself too fully. Partly for the same reason I think, she fails to be an artist: she does not live at all upon instinct. The artist is part of him a drifter, at the mercy of impressions, and another part of him allows this to happen for the sake of making use of the unhappy creature. But in Edith the division is merely the rational, the cold and detached part of the artist, itself divided. Her material, her experience that is, is already a mental product, already digested by reason. Hence Edith (I only at this moment arrive at understanding) is really the most orderly person in existence, and the most rational.

Nothing ever happens to her; everything that happens is her own doing."

"And hence also," continued Appleplex, catching up the thread, "Edith is the least detached of all persons, since to be detached is to be detached from one's self, to stand by and criticise coldly one's own passions and vicissitudes. But in Edith the critic is coaching the combatant."

"Edith is not unhappy."

"She is dissatisfied, perhaps."

"But again I say, she is not tragic: she is too rational. And in her career there is no progression, no decline or degeneration. Her condition is once and for always. There is and will be no catastrophe.

"But I am tired. I still wonder what Edith and Mrs. Howexden have in common. This invites the consideration (you may not perceive the connection) of Sets and Society, a subject which we can pursue tomorrow night."

Appleplex looked a little embarrassed. "I am dining with Mrs. Howexden," he said. "But I will reflect upon the topic before I see you again."

www.ingramcontent.com/pod-product-compliance
Lightning Source LLC
LaVergne TN
LVHW091008080826
845145LV00003B/1183

* 9 7 8 1 6 2 7 3 0 0 3 9 1 *